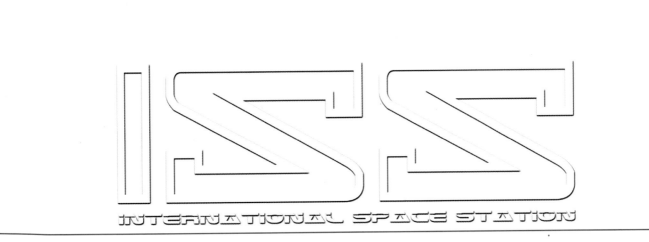

INTERNATIONAL SPACE STATION

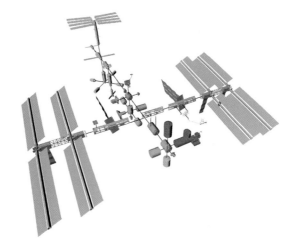

Author: David Jefferis, MBIS
Illustrator: Sebastian Quigley
Consultant: Mat Irvine, FBIS

Created and produced by Firecrest Books Ltd
in association with Alpha Communications

Published by Tangerine Press, an imprint of Scholastic Inc;
557 Broadway, New York, NY 10012

10 9 8 7 6 5 4 3 2 1

ISBN 0-439-43042-9

Printed and bound in Italy
First printing September 2002

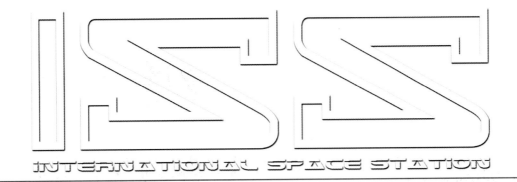

ISS
INTERNATIONAL SPACE STATION

DAVID JEFFERIS
Illustrated by SEBASTIAN QUIGLEY

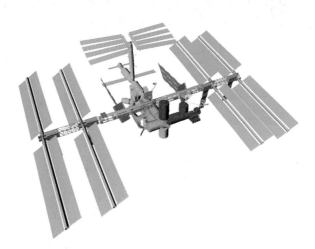

tangerine Press®

Tangerine Press and associated logo and
design are trademarks of Scholastic Inc.

Publishing Consultant
Peter Sackett

Designer and Art Director
Phil Jacobs

Editor
Norman Barrett

Color separation by
SC (Sang Choy) International Pte Ltd.

Printed in Italy by
Grafica Editoriale Printing SRL

Acknowledgments
We wish to thank all those individuals and organizations
that have helped create this publication:
Agencia Espacial Brasileira, Alenia Aerospazio,
Arianespace, Boeing Corporation,
European Space Agency (ESA), Marshall Space Flight Center,
National Aeronautics & Space Administration (NASA),
National Space Development Agency of Japan (NASDA)

Photographs courtesy:
NASA, ESA, NASDA, David Jefferis

CONTENTS

THE STATION

The ISS, or International Space Station (also known as Alpha), is the biggest human-made object in space. The ISS circles the Earth once every 80 minutes and presently carries a crew of three. But the ISS gets bigger as parts are added, and planners hope that, in the future, crews of up to seven may be able to stay there.

A robot arm is used to manipulate objects near the ISS.

Can-shaped modules all use similar fittings, and are sized to fit in a Space Shuttle's cargo bay.

The first two ISS modules were linked in 1998.

THE INTERNATIONAL SPACE STATION is designed to be a huge laboratory in space. The first units, or modules, were placed in orbit in late 1998, when the entire ISS was a little bigger than a freight truck. The first crew went aboard in October 2000, and since then the ISS has grown steadily, as parts have been added.

When fully built, the ISS will be a space-giant, measuring 290 ft. (88.4 m) long, with huge solar-panel "wings" stretching 356 ft. (108.5 m). The finished ISS will be a large chunk of hardware – on Earth it would weigh 446.4 long tons (453.5 tonnes), and cover an area the size of a football field!

Modules carry equipment for a wide range of experiments.

In the future, streamlined spacecraft like this may be used, as well as, US Shuttles and Russian craft.

The backbone of the ISS is this central truss. Modules and panels are attached to it.

Three-seat Russian craft also dock with the ISS and can be used as an emergency lifeboat.

Living areas are filled with air at the same pressure as on Earth.

Track of ISS over the Earth

The ISS circles the Earth at an average height of 220 mi. (407 km). The path of the ISS takes it over much of our planet, giving crews a grandstand view of the continents and oceans below.

SPACE TRUCK

The US Space Shuttle is the heavy-hauler craft that takes major components to the ISS. Shuttles and their crews have been hard at work on construction duty since 1998.

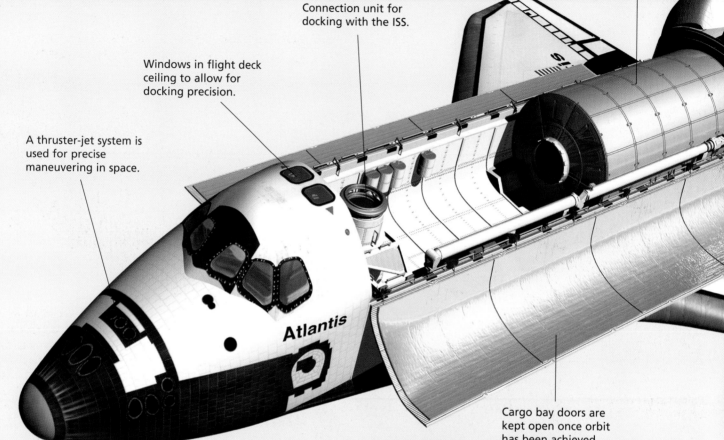

Modules on their way to the ISS are stored in the cargo bay.

Connection unit for docking with the ISS.

Windows in flight deck ceiling to allow for docking precision.

A thruster-jet system is used for precise maneuvering in space.

Atlantis

Cargo bay doors are kept open once orbit has been achieved.

THE US SPACE SHUTTLE IS THE BIGGEST CRAFT to visit the ISS. It is used to deliver ISS construction components and supplies, as well as to take crews back and forth. The crewed part of the shuttle system is the orbiter shown here. At take-off, the orbiter is attached to two solid-rocket boosters (SRBs), and a huge external fuel tank (ET). But these are all left behind when their fuel is spent. Only the orbiter visits the ISS.

There are several orbiters, and they take turns visiting the ISS, as well as being used for other crewed space missions, such as launching satellites or servicing the Hubble Space Telescope. As spacecraft go, an orbiter is quite roomy, with accommodations for up to seven astronauts at a time. Most importantly for the ISS, the orbiter was built as a "space truck" – it has a massive cargo bay that is 60 ft. (18.29 m) long and 15 ft. (4.57 m) wide.

Final approach to the ISS is slow and careful. The cargo bay doors are open as they have radiators to cool the craft in the glare of sunlight.

An orbiter glides in to land, usually at the Kennedy Space Center in Florida. The wheels are lowered just a few seconds before touchdown. On the runway, a parachute is released from the tail to help slow the orbiter.

Small tail rockets come into use after the external tank's fuel is exhausted.

AFTER A MISSION, Shuttle orbiters are flown back to Earth. The first part of a return involves hitting the upper atmosphere at about 17,300 mph (28,000 km/h), which causes heat through friction. Parts of the nose and wings may reach 3000°F (1650°C).

Three main engines are used for take-off, fueled from the external tank.

Ailerons and a tail rudder are used to steer during landing.

Orbiters are covered with heatproof materials.

For take-off, an orbiter is linked to two solid-rocket boosters and an external fuel tank (ET). The boosters fall away when their fuel is used up, after 123 seconds. The orbiter's own main engines run on fuel from the ET most of the way into space.

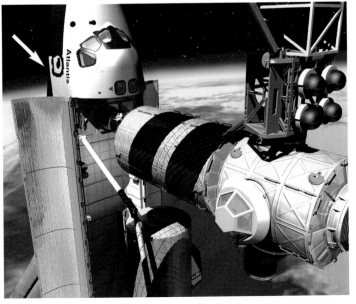

Orbiters dock with the ISS by means of a unit just behind the flight deck. The side door (arrowed) is used before take-off and after landing.

Small thrusters at the nose and tail are for changing an orbiter's angle, or making fine positional adjustments.

Russian spacecraft come in two similar types, the computer-controlled Progress space freighter (shown here) and the crewed Soyuz, which carries up to three astronauts. The spacecraft design has been developed and improved over many years – the first Soyuz flew long ago in 1967.

Supplies are also carried in the center module. This part of the Progress can also return safely to Earth, with materials such as photographic film or completed experiments.

Rear section of the Progress spacecraft is the equipment module. It has rocket engines and fuel for accurate space maneuvers, such as docking with the ISS.

Pairs of small rocket motors, for adjusting the spacecraft's speed and angle in space.

Fold-out radio antenna.

RUSSIAN SPACECRAFT ON ISS MISSIONS are launched from Earth on top of huge Proton rockets, from Baikonur, Russia's giant cosmodrome in Siberia.

Soyuz and Progress spacecraft are built for different jobs, but have the same layout. There are three main modules. The *equipment module* carries rocket motors and extending solar wings, which supply electricity in space. The *nose module* contains the equipment needed to join up safely with one of the docking ports of the ISS. The *center module* is the main cargo section in the Progress and the crew compartment of the Soyuz. It is also the only module to return to Earth – both nose and tail modules burn up in the intense heat generated when they re-enter the atmosphere at nearly 5 miles per second (8 km/sec).

Landing back on Earth is very different than the shuttle orbiter's aircraft-style approach. Instead, the last moments of a Russian space mission are spent floating down to the ground under a set of huge parachutes.

A docking approach to the ISS is an extremely accurate flight maneuver.

After a Progress mission to the ISS, the nose module can be filled with station waste. It's a space "garbage can" that burns up in the atmosphere.

Progress docks with the ISS nose-first, in an automatic approach.

Fresh supplies include all sorts of things, such as air and food. Materials for science experiments are also carried regularly.

Here a crewed Soyuz TM spacecraft is docked to the ISS Zvezda module during a visit in 2001. You can just see the wing of a shuttle beyond it.

Antenna used during docking approach.

Attitude jets to control the angle of the spacecraft.

Back of solar panels, which provide electric power in space. They are folded up during launch, and extend when the craft is in orbit.

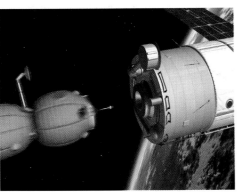

The metal nose probe is aimed at a matching slot in the ISS docking hatch.

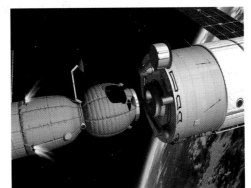

A last-moment correction burn from the motors brings the spacecraft to the hatch.

Spacecraft and ISS are now firmly connected together in what is called a "hard dock."

BIGGER AND BIGGER

Space construction of the ISS started in 1998, when the Russian-built Zarya module was placed in orbit. Building up the station is expected to last until about 2006, when the last parts of the station should be completed.

The Zarya (Sunrise) control module was carried aboard a Proton rocket from Russia's Baikonur Cosmodrome, in November 1998. The 42,600 lbs. (19.62 tonnes) Zarya was built in Russia, its job to control the ISS's angle in space, as well as looking after communications and electric power. Here US astronaut James Newman floats outside Zarya on his third spacewalk during an ISS assembly mission in December 1998.

Radiator

The long Integrated Truss Assembly is the backbone of the ISS.

Modules are joined together by 16 connecting bolts, to make sure there is a good seal. This is so air cannot leak out into space.

EVERYTHING ON THE ISS IS CARRIED FROM EARTH aboard three types of spacecraft, the US Space Shuttle and the Russian Progress and Soyuz. As planned, it will take 43 space missions to complete the ISS, by 2005-2006.

The station's "backbone" will be the Integrated Truss Assembly (ITA). When finished, this will consist of 10 segments, joined together like a long girder. The simple look of the Truss hides its importance – wires and cables carry electricity and information to all parts of the ISS. Canada's robotic arm and hand will move along tracks. The Truss will house batteries, radiators, antennas, gyros, and other equipment.

Some early space station designs had a wheel shape, which could spin slowly to give crews a sensation of weight on board. The ISS is much simpler – it had to be made of modules that could fit inside a shuttle's cargo bay.

MOST SHUTTLE TRIPS to the ISS carry extra parts, for building the ISS is a long job. Joining a new component to the ISS usually calls for robot arms to move large parts, while astronauts in spacesuits go outside in an EVA (Extravehicular Activity) to make final connections and to test that everything is working correctly.

The completed ISS is HUGE – it will be the biggest human-made object in space, compared with a 360 ft. (110 m) football field.

Zarya module

Total volume inside the finished ISS is about 43,000 cu. ft. (1,218 cu m), spread across six science modules. This is a similar volume to the cabins and cargo space of a large jetliner, such as a Boeing 747.

Radiators release heat from the ISS into space. They are part of the thermal control system (TCS).

The total area covered by the solar panels is 27,000 sq. ft. (2,500 sq m). On Earth, the electric power system equipment would weigh 150,000 lbs. (70 tonnes).

13

POWER SUPPLY

Huge solar-panel "wings" supply power for the space station. They work by converting the energy in sunlight to electricity, which is essential for running the station's many systems.

ELECTRICITY IS VITAL for running the ISS. It is used to keep the air and water systems running, for pumping liquid, and for lighting. Other uses include heating meals and shaving, and of course, all the station's computers and radios depend on electricity.

The solar-panel wings, called "photovoltaic arrays," generate the power. They are made of special silicon materials that convert the sunlight's energy into electricity. But power also has to be stored regularly. When the ISS passes into the Earth's shadow, power comes from batteries that have been charged in the sunshine.

Solar arrays are turned to face the Sun as the ISS circles in its orbit around the Earth.

When the solar-array system is finished, it will have 262,400 individual solar cells.

THREE SPACE POWER SYSTEMS

Fuel cells are used on the space shuttle to make electricity from oxygen and hydrogen.

Nuclear generators are needed on space probes that travel far from the Sun.

ISS batteries are recharged when the station is in sunlight. New ones are needed every five years.

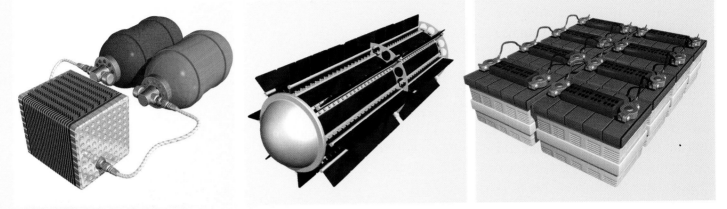

SWITCHING BETWEEN SOLAR POWER AND BATTERIES takes place twice every orbit – because the ISS spends up to 36 minutes in the Earth's shadow, when the panels generate little or no power. Switching was quite a challenge for the power system's designers, because many machines depend on a very smooth flow of power. Some experiments could be ruined if there is even a moment's interruption.

Batteries can also get very hot, so the ISS has radiators to get rid of the heat into space. Yet another problem is the strong electric field that surrounds the solar panels. Without a gadget called a circuit isolation device (CID), a spacewalking astronaut could get shocked!

Main solar arrays

This view of the ISS shows the full extent of the finished solar panels.

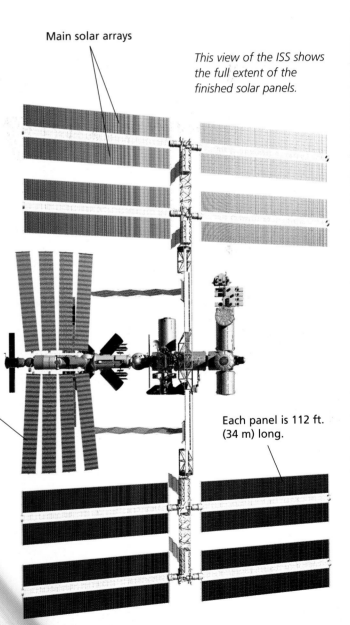

Small solar arrays

Each panel is 112 ft. (34 m) long.

ROBOT ARM

The ISS uses a long robotic arm, called the Canadarm 2. It is a larger version of the Canadian arm used on the US Space Shuttles, and was installed on the ISS in 2001.

THE CANADARM 2 CAME FROM EARTH in the cargo bay of the Space Shuttle Endeavour. It was attached to the ISS by a three-person shuttle team that included two spacewalkers, Chris Hadfield and Scott Parazynski. The arm is called a "robot," though it is under the control of human operators using workstations in the ISS.

Canadarm 2 has several "elbows" for flexibility, and can do many jobs that would otherwise have to be carried out by astronauts. It helps keep astronauts safe by avoiding unnecessary spacewalks.

On Earth the complete arm weighs 3,620 lbs. (1,642 kg). It is a total of 57.7 ft. (17.59 m) long. And it cost over $600 million to develop.

Several rotating joints allow the arm to be very flexible.

Pressure sensors on the hand's fingers give operators in the ISS a sense of feel.

Joints give the hand great flexibility.

Cameras and lights give operators a close-up view.

A multi-window cupola is planned for the ISS in 2005. One of the arm's workstations will be inside, from where the operator will get a clear all-round view.

THE ARM'S MOBILE BASE SYSTEM was also made in Canada. The arm attaches to the base system, which can move back and forth about the station on rails, much like a small truck. Using this, an operator can move the arm from job to job quickly and easily. The arm's complicated-looking "hand" is called the Special Purpose Dexterous Manipulator (SPDM). It is equipped with lights, video cameras, and various holders and clips for tools, such as drills and screwdrivers.

Mission specialist Scott Parazynski carries out a spacewalk at the ISS. He is sorting out connections in the complex cable systems at the base of the Canadarm 2, during the 2001 delivery mission. Here the spindly arm is folded up, like the legs of a giant spider.

A WORLDWIDE SPACE PROJECT

Building the International Space Station is the work of thousands of people across the world. They come from countries that include the United States, Russia, Canada, Japan, Brazil, and the European countries that are members of the European Space Agency (ESA).

BUILDING THE ISS IS A MEGA-PROJECT that is also mega-expensive – the United States space station budget for 2002 alone was over $2 billion, and altogether the ISS will cost more than $30 billion. However, compared with everyday spending, the station does not seem quite so pricey. For example, in the same year, Americans spent $31 billion on airline flights, $66 billion on tobacco products, and nearly $100 billion on new automobiles!

Even so, the cost of the ISS is easier to spread across several nations, and this is where the international side of the project comes into its own. The Russians have their own part of the ISS and regularly send supplies. And a three-seat Soyuz spacecraft is always docked on the station, as a space lifeboat. If there is a real emergency, the crew can climb aboard the Soyuz, and fly safely back to Earth. In Europe, eleven countries of the European Space Agency (ESA) are working on the ISS. Teams are busy developing flight hardware for the ISS, and Europeans are eager to fly into space. Russian Soyuz spacecraft fly regularly with mixed crews, including Claudie Haigneré from France, who was the first European woman to visit the ISS, in 2001.

But the planners did not expect the ISS to become a space hotel. Some American officials were not pleased when Russia announced that American Dennis Tito would fly to the ISS in April 2001. In fact, his visit drew lots of publicity and criticism about the ISS not being a space hotel!

The Russian Zarya module was launched by Proton rocket from the Baikonur Cosmodrome in 1998. The Zarya is carried in the dark-painted upper section of the Proton.

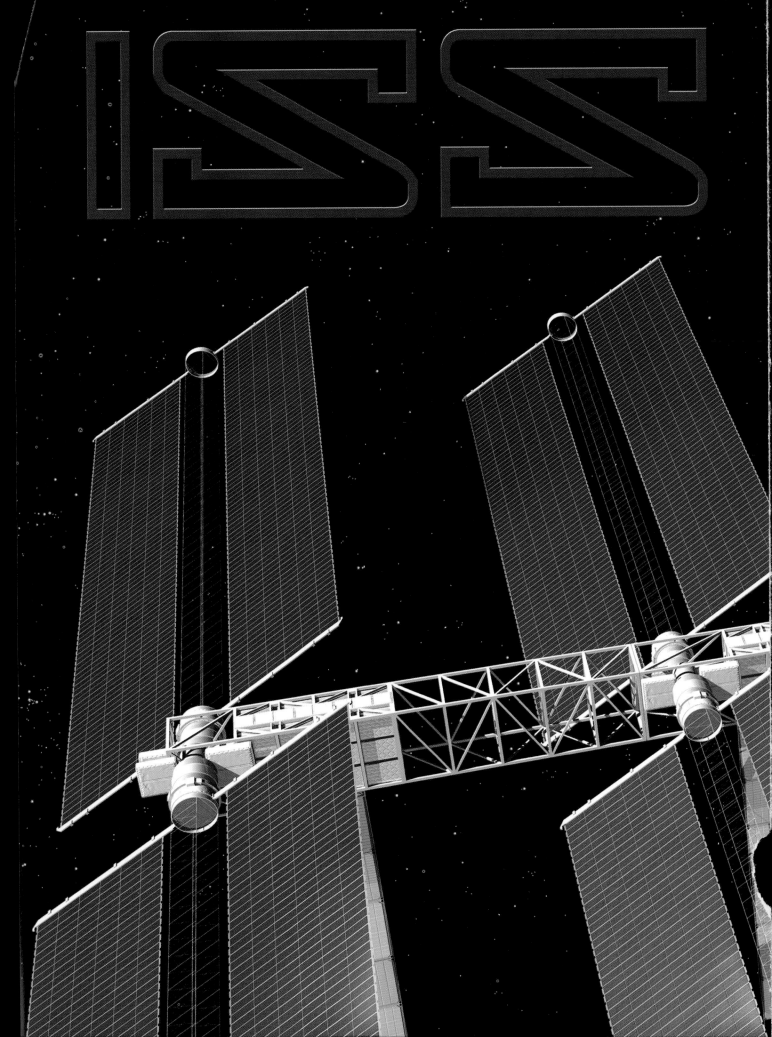

For the United States, one big difference between the ISS and earlier stations is that the ISS is put together piece-by-piece. In the 1970s, the US Skylab was a large rocket fuel tank fitted with living quarters. When the fuel was used up, the tank could be converted to a space home very quickly. The ISS is different – joining all the modules together is a years-long job, involving many flights by US Space Shuttles and Russian rockets. But there are benefits to this approach, for the end-result will be a bigger and more capable space station, built to last for many years. Spacewalking astronauts from many countries can experience assembling and maintaining equipment in the difficult conditions of space. This may be useful in the future, if companies decide to build space factories in orbit, for ISS crews will have solved many construction problems. And one day human missions that go farther than Earth's orbit may be planned. By 2010, there may be missions to return to the Moon or perhaps even a flight to the planet Mars. If so, the ISS and its crews will have played a key part in finding out how to live and work safely in space for long periods.

Spacewalking is an important part of building the ISS. Here astronaut James Newman checks module fittings as he floats weightless in space. Lights either side of his helmet help when the ISS goes into Earth's shadow.

WHO MAKES WHAT

- United States: central truss, main solar arrays, Destiny laboratory module, Unity node 1, US habitation module, thermal control system

- Russia: Zarya control module, Zvezda service module, universal docking module with living quarters, two research modules with solar arrays

- Japan: Kibo module, exposed facility, robotic arm

- Canada: Canadarm 2

- Brazil: express pallet

- Italy: multi-purpose logistics modules

- European Space Agency (Belgium, Denmark, France, Germany, Italy, Netherlands, Norway, Spain, Sweden, Switzerland, United Kingdom): Columbus laboratory module, Jules Verne automated transfer vehicle, cupola observation dome, connector nodes 2 and 3

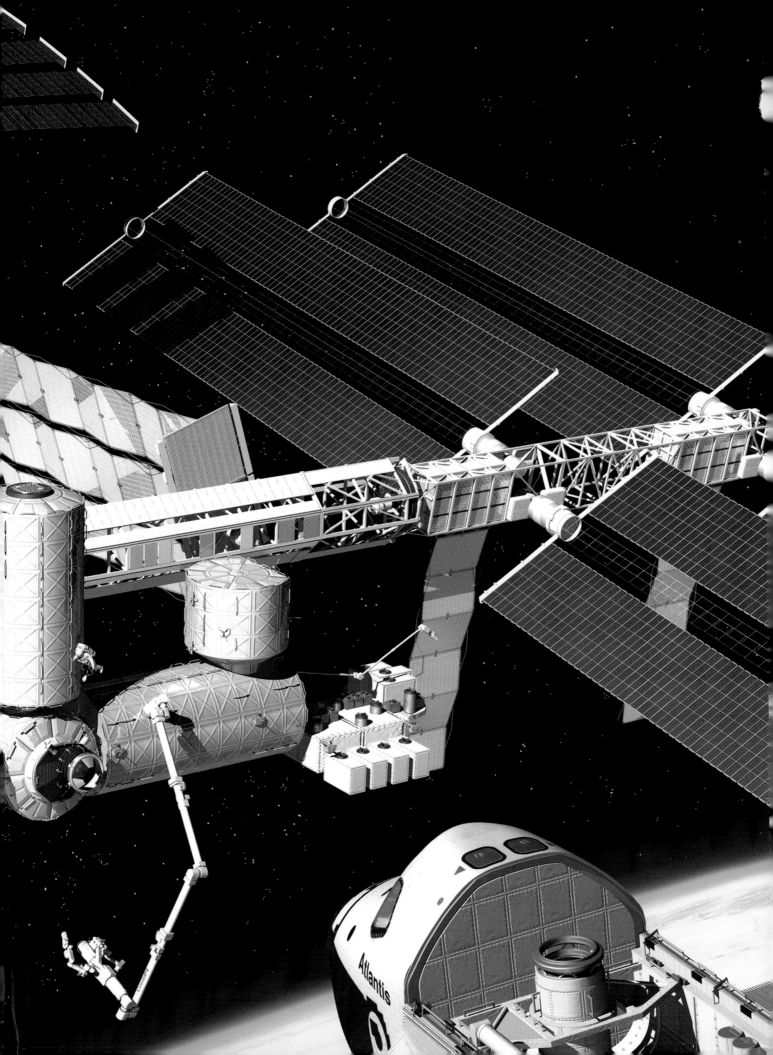

DESTINY LABORATORY

The Destiny laboratory is the centerpiece for United States research on the ISS. It was launched aboard the Shuttle Atlantis in 2001, and should give a steady stream of useful science information for more than ten years.

Destiny is 14 ft. (4.3 m) across.

Criss-cross waffle pattern in the aluminum shell gives it extra strength.

Destiny is attached to the far end of this early ISS module link-up.

End cone has a hatch for astronauts.

DESTINY IS AN ALUMINUM CAN 28 ft. (8.5 m) long. Inside, there is room for 24 equipment racks – 13 of these are for experiments, the rest are used for power, cooling, and life-support systems.

The 32,000 lbs. (14.5-tonne) laboratory also has the best window in space. The 20 in. (50.8 cm) WORF (Window Observational Research Facility) is made of a top-quality optical glass. On Earth, a double-glazed window usually has two panes of glass, each about 0.1 in. (2.5 mm) thick. The WORF has four panes of glass, from 0.5 to 1.25 in. (13-32 mm) thick, plus a metal shutter for protection when nobody is looking out.

These photographs show the grandstand view of our planet that ISS gives its crews, looking down from an average height of 220 mi. (350 km). Viewing through the high-quality glass of WORF, a good camera can show tiny details on the ground quite easily.

This swirling thunderstorm was the first picture of Earth taken from the ISS.

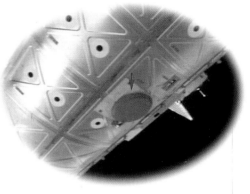

This video still from outside the ISS shows Destiny from below. The red arrow shows where the WORF is fitted.

You can just see the pyramids of Giza (arrowed) in this view of Egypt.

When the WORF is not being used, a metal shutter covers it for protection from space dust or other damage.

Astronauts can check on river-valley erosion in the Andes Mountains of South America.

Russian cosmonaut Sergei Krikalev looks through the finished WORF, ready for a photo-shoot with his camera.

The Columbus laboratory module, Europe's biggest contribution to the ISS, is due to be launched by a space shuttle in 2004. The Jules Verne automated transfer vehicle (ATV) is a computerized cargo freighter which should be launched by 2005.

Columbus has fittings for outside experiments.

Columbus is made of aluminum, up to 0.25 in. (6.5 mm) thick at the ends.

Computers provide links with ground controllers.

Equipment rack

Grab rails for astronauts outside the ISS

Up to three people at a time can work in Columbus.

Columbus is 22.5 ft. (6.86 m) long and 13.6 ft. (4.15 m) in diameter.

THE COLUMBUS SPACE LABORATORY IS BEING BUILT by a group of European companies headed by the German firm Astrium. Columbus will be filled with rows of standard-size racks, each packed with high-tech equipment that includes video and communications links to scientists on Earth. Columbus is designed to work for at least ten years in space, and during this time thousands of experiments will be carried out.

 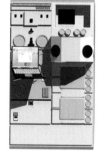 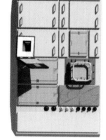 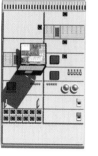

Columbus has room for up to 10 slot-in payload racks. These are designed to be mostly automatic or controlled by science teams on Earth. ISS crews may help out from time to time, or sort out any problems with the equipment. As planned, information from the experiments will be published by the European Space Agency in a growing computer database over the years to come.

The first four racks include experiments in biology, physiology, fluids, and materials.

Solar panels provide power to rechargeable batteries so that ATV can work in the Earth's shadow.

Cargo area in the front half of the ATV

Small attitude jets change angle and direction of ATV.

Four thruster rockets for main maneuvers in orbit

Docking probe

Once a trip to the ISS is complete, the ATV can be used as a flying trash can. Filled with up to 12,000 lbs. (5.5 tonnes) of waste from the station, the ATV will burn up during re-entry into the Earth's atmosphere. Any surviving parts will crash into the ocean.

The ATV will be carried in the upper section of an Ariane V rocket.

THE JULES VERNE automated transfer vehicle is built by another group of European companies, this time headed by European Aeronautic Defense and Space Company (EADS), which makes Airbus airliners. Fully loaded on the launch pad, an ATV will weigh over 45,000 lbs. (20.5 tonnes), of which nearly 17,000 lbs. (7.7 tonnes) can be cargo supplies for the ISS. A typical load could be a mixture of water and air tanks, plus assorted items for experiments. The ATV may also have another important job – once docked to the ISS, its thruster rockets will be able to push the ISS into a slightly different orbit. When a mission is finished, the ATV will detach from the ISS, and head back to earth. But it won't be reused – it will burn up in the atmosphere.

The Ariane V is Europe's biggest rocket. It is launched from Europe's launch site in Kourou, French Guiana, South America. Present plans call for about one ATV mission a year to the ISS.

Dozens of companies across Europe are developing various items for the ISS. The European Space Agency (ESA) is in charge of their efforts.

The ends of the 34.5 ft. (10.5 m) long Euro-arm are interchangeable. Each can act as a "hand," or a "shoulder" base. The hand can swing at a top speed of about 8 inches per second (200 mm/sec), and can be placed to an accuracy of about 0.125 in. (3 mm).

Arm sections are made of strong, but light, carbon-fiber, with aluminum ends to meet the joints.

THE FOKKER COMPANY IN THE NETHERLANDS leads a team of European companies that is making another robotic arm for the ISS. The Euro-arm is due to be launched after 2004, and will be attached to the Russian-built science platform. The arm will be controlled from inside or outside the station, using two different control panels.

The arm handles loads weighing up to 17,500 lbs. (8 tonnes) on Earth.

One of the earliest parts of the ISS was the Russian Zvezda service module, which was launched in 2000. Its DMS-R computers were made in Europe, and provide navigation and guidance control for the entire ISS.

Metal screens are swung over the windows for protection when they are not in use.

In the factory, the cupola weighs nearly 4,000 lbs. (1.8 tonnes).

The Node 2 and Node 3 modules are each 20.4 ft. (6.2 m) long, and have hatches that join to other ISS modules, like the click-together parts of a Lego® set. The Nodes are made of aluminum and, like other ISS components, are covered with a "bumper" system for protection against collision with space objects.

Grab rails provide hand-holds for astronauts on Extravehicular Activity (EVA) missions.

EUROPEAN TEAMS ARE HARD AT WORK on other parts of the ISS too. The Alenia company of Italy heads a team building the can-shaped Node 2 and Node 3 modules. These will be used to join other modules to each other, using a system of circular airtight hatches.

Alenia is also in charge of making an observation dome, called the cupola. This will be a small six-sided room with an all-round space view. From inside, an astronaut will be able to look through a circle of six windows, plus a round porthole overhead. Jobs in the cupola will range from observing approaching spacecraft, controlling the station's robotic arm, or studying space objects such as the Earth, Sun, stars, and planets.

The Node 3 module will be launched in 2005. Node 3 will have equipment to process used air, dirty water, and toilet waste.

Each node is protected from damage from high-speed space particles by 98 panels.

Node 2 is an electronic "information exchange" between the ISS Truss and other modules. The main robotic arm can also be fixed to it.

The cupola is due to be launched by a Space Shuttle in 2005. It is made of lightweight aluminum and measures 9.7 ft. (2.96 m) across. Inside, the cupola features a computer workstation, lights, and window heaters. Foot restraints prevent an astronaut from floating around.

Connections with systems inside the Node modules give the cupola an air supply, electrical power for computers, lighting, heating, and cooling.

きぼう

Kibo, or "Hope," is the name of the Japanese Experimental Module (JEM). It is an ISS research unit built to hold up to four scientist-astronauts to work at a time.

Experiment Logistics Module

Kibo's Pressurized Module (PM) is more than 36 ft. (11 m) long, about the size of a tourist bus. Here it is shown during construction in a Japanese factory.

Main module provides a comfortable atmosphere for up to four scientist-astronauts.

Ten racks of instruments can be used for experiments. Another 13 racks are used for storage and running the module's systems.

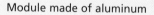

Module made of aluminum

Handrails

THE KIBO SCIENTIFIC RESEARCH MODULE is made of four main sections. The biggest part is the Pressurized Module (PM), which is an air-filled tube designed to be a comfortable place to work. Joined to the top is the Experiment Logistics Module (ELM), which carries scientific supplies. At one end of the PM is an open pallet system, often called the "back porch." Here experiments can be placed by Kibo's robot arm, where they are exposed to the vacuum of space. An airlock allows the arm to move experiments in and out of the PM when required.

Container for experiments

Japan is also making a 10 ft. (3 m) wide centrifuge. It is designed to spin boxes of experiments around and around. The faster they spin, the more they seem to weigh, so scientists can check how various things (especially plants and small animals) behave in these conditions.

Cargo sections are in the front half of the HTV

Person to scale

HTV can carry cargo weighing up to 15,500 lbs. (7 tonnes).

Japan's HII Transfer Vehicle (HTV) is being developed as an uncrewed space freighter. Unlike the Russian Progress, which docks directly into an ISS hatch, HTV will come to a halt near the ISS, then be brought in close by robot arm.

Kibo has its own 32.5 ft. (9.79 m) robot arm.

Airlock

Container system for experiments

Radio antenna

Camera

Equipment can be inspected and changed by the robot arm.

Japan's astronauts started advanced training for the Kibo module at the Tsukuba Space Center, in December 2001. Here Nauko Sumino checks out a spacesuit. The training facilities at Tsukuba include a big underwater tank, in which astronauts can practice operations such as spacewalks using a mock-up of Kibo. Floating underwater is a lot like being weightless. Tests like this are used by American and Russian astronauts, too. Divers in scuba gear are on hand to help, and to rescue in case a spacesuit springs a leak.

RESEARCH PANORAMA

Research is the aim of the ISS, and planners believe that, in its first 10 years of operation, crews should be able to carry out thousands of experiments – and that does not include work done by automated equipment.

LIFE SCIENCES

Damaged cell

Life science researchers investigate how being in space affects living things – and it's mostly bad news, because bones become brittle, and too much radiation causes cancers and destroys cells. The "Phantom Torso" shown at right is a way to check on the space environment – it is packed with sensors to check radiation damage.

EARTH SCIENCES

The ISS orbits around the Earth once every 80 minutes, so it makes a good platform from which to study our planet. ISS crews can assess world-wide weather patterns and monitor long-term changes, such as pollution and global warming.

Plumes of smoke and ash rise from the Mt. Etna volcano, during an eruption in 2001.

SPACE SCIENCES

Orbiting high above Earth's atmosphere, the ISS is a good place for an observatory. Equipment on board gives crews a chance to study space objects, such as this exploding star.

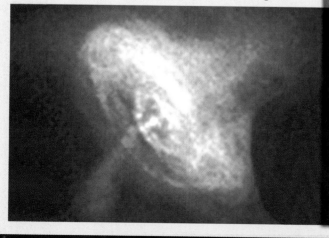

SPACE PRODUCTS

Many drug experiments will be carried out in space, such as finding a cure for diabetes. Insulin crystals can be grown larger and purer in space than down on Earth.

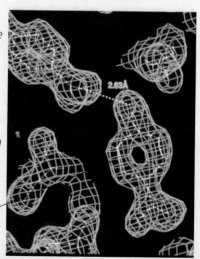

Computer display shows insulin molecules grown in space.

MICROGRAVITY RESEARCH

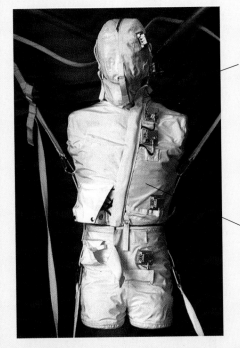

Phantom torso is the same size and shape as a typical human.

Sensors are placed in the body in the same places as the heart, lungs, and other sensitive organs.

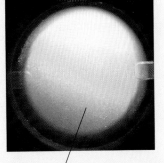

An ISS experiment with a colloid, a liquid (such as paint or ink) with particles suspended inside.

The ISS is a nearly weightless environment, in which objects weigh about one-billionth as much as they do on Earth. Many things behave differently in microgravity. For example, hot air does not rise, so if you light·a match, the flame burns in a sphere until the nearby oxygen is used up. Air bubbles can be sprayed into hot metal to make a strong lightweight metal foam when it cools. Other research points to new kinds of paints and inks, with ultra-fine mixtures.

TECHNOLOGY

The Materials ISS Experiment (MISSE) aims to find better things from which to make spacecraft. Various samples (metals, plastics, and many others) are left for up to three years on a special rack just outside the Quest airlock module. There they have to survive the fierce heat of direct sun, icy cold in the shadows, and erosion by space dust. The best materials may be used in future.

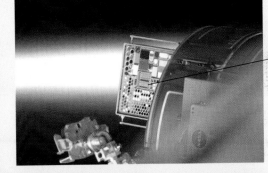

The first MISSE rack was attached to the ISS in August 2001.

Flying anything into space is expensive, so experiments are always designed to be as small and lightweight as possible. Here a Russian cosmonaut checks out a micro-laboratory that produces an anti-cancer drug. If results work as well as hoped, the medicine could be made in large quantities for use by patients across the world.

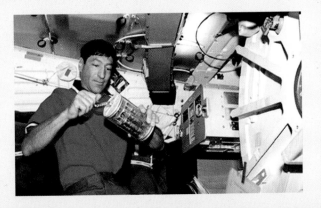

SPACESUIT

If an astronaut needs to go outside the ISS, wearing a spacesuit is vital. A spacesuit is like a one-person spacecraft, with equipment that is designed to keep an astronaut safe in the deadly space environment.

The helmet faceplate is coated with a thin layer of gold. This cuts down on the intense glare and heat from the Sun

A one-piece "Snoopy" hat contains a microphone and headset for talking to crew on board the ISS or a visiting spacecraft.

EARLY AMERICAN SPACESUITS were modified from jet-fighter pilots' flight gear. Flying in a single-seated Mercury spacecraft, the first US astronauts wore an inner suit made of nylon fabric, covered with an outer suit of aluminized material. Suit design has changed for new missions, including the Apollo Moon flights of 1969-72. ISS spacesuits are made with space construction in mind, as building the ISS involves 1,200 hours of planned spacewalks. Heating and cooling systems keep an astronaut comfortable, while communications gear allows a spacewalker to talk to the ISS crew during an EVA, which typically lasts four hours or more. Air supplies are carried in the bulky backpack. ISS suits also have a lighting system, because the station spends some time every orbit in the Earth's shadow.

Early US astronauts show off their shiney silver suits.

Astronaut clips tether to one of the many handrails on the ISS.

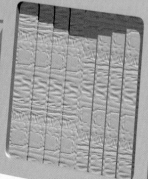

Spacesuits like this were worn to explore the Moon, during the US Apollo missions, from 1969 to 1972. These suits were bulkier and took more time to put on than modern types.

Lights and cameras

Astronauts practice repair and construction jobs in huge water tanks on Earth before doing them for real in space.

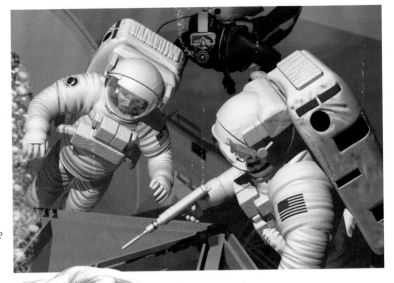

ISS assembly power tool

EVA PRESS

Control panel for the suit's life-support systems.

Backpack has life-support equipment for up to eight hours.

Pipes from Portable Life-Support System (PLSS) in the backpack.

Suit weighs about 250 lbs. (113 kg) on Earth. It is designed to last at least eight years.

This spacesuit is made in top and bottom halves, joined at the waist by a sealed connecting ring. An astronaut wears a cooling garment underneath, as well as helmet, gloves, and backpack. It is a big improvement over Apollo-type suits, which were less flexible to wear.

A shuttle flight to the ISS usually lasts 10-14 days. If a construction trip is planned, the cargo bay may be filled completely with an ISS payload. But, if there is room, the shuttle may carry a satellite for launching during the mission. Once docked to the ISS, shuttle astronauts (up to seven can fly at once) can visit the three crew members on the ISS.

A shuttle astronaut's view of the ISS not long before docking. It's hard to believe the two spacecraft are covering a distance of about 290 mi. (467 km) every minute.

BUILDING AND MAINTAINING THE ISS involves dozens of flights by the US Space Shuttle and the Russian Progress and Soyuz. Flights are split three ways. (1) The shuttle takes up large modules and exchanges crew – when docked, its seven-person team joins the three-person ISS team. (2) The latest Progress is an automatic supply craft that takes up supplies and can return materials to Earth. (3) Soyuz is the "space taxi" and "lifeboat." It takes three people, so can carry a crew, and – most importantly – stays docked with the ISS for long periods of time. While docked, it is available for use as a lifeboat back to Earth, if anything goes seriously wrong with the station.

ISS commander Yuri Onufrienko waits by the hatch, so he can welcome the shuttle crew when the spacecraft has docked.

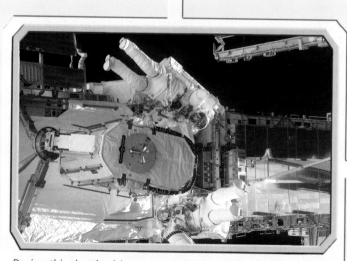

During this shuttle visit, astronauts make a spacewalk to assemble sections of the ISS. Colored bands identify each astronaut.

James Voss uses computer and TV equipment to control the robot arm during an assembly job.

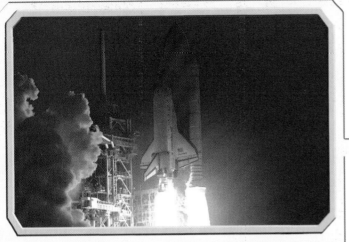

The Space Shuttle lifts off from Kennedy Space Center in Florida. It goes from zero to over 17,000 mph (28,000 km/h) in eight minutes.

Once in space, orbiter and crew float weightless. On the flight deck, checks are made that the spacecraft is on course for the station.

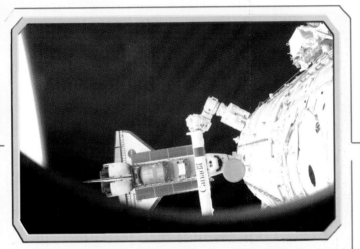

Here the Shuttle Endeavour is seen from inside the ISS, as it drifts slowly by. In front, you can see the Canadian robot arm.

Now the ISS is just a short distance ahead. Nearest the camera is a three-seat Soyuz space taxi (arrowed) already docked to the station.

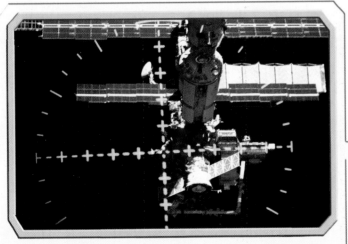

After the visit, the shuttle undocks from the ISS and moves slowly away. A sighting "cross-hair" helps the crew be precise in flying.

Mission's end – the shuttle comes in to land at 215 mph (346 km/h). A parachute opens behind the tail fin to help slow it down.

LIVING IN SPACE

Living on the ISS is very different than being on Earth. But some things stay the same – apart from their work, ISS crews also need regular exercise, have some time off, sleep well, and eat the right foods.

ISS CREWS EAT THREE MEALS A DAY in a range of foods that is balanced for their likes, dislikes, and physical size – bigger people get more to eat. Mexican tortillas are a better space food than normal bread, because there are fewer crumbs. Crumbs could float into delicate electronic equipment, get stuck in air vents, or, even worse, go up an astronaut's nose. Salt and pepper are supplied as ready-mixed liquids, because they cannot be shaken over food – the grains would float away. But plenty of things can be eaten normally, such as nuts, many fruits, and chocolate brownies. And the ISS has an oven, so hot meals are a regular part of the menu. Drinks are sealed in bottles. Like crumbs, spilled drinks can be a safety hazard, as well as a nuisance, for a globule of liquid floating into an electrical system can easily cause a fire. After meals, astronauts gather up any waste food and packaging, then squeeze it tightly in a trash compactor. Later on, stored waste leaves the ISS on board a Progress cargo ship or a Space Shuttle.

You can buy some space food in science shops. These freeze-dried strawberries weigh very little and keep for years in their sealed packet. No water is needed when you want to eat them – simply pop a strawberry into your mouth, and saliva does the job.

The most obvious difference between living on Earth, and living on the ISS, is you float in free-fall. In space, there is no "up" or "down," as shown by these astronauts in the Destiny laboratory. Most space travelers are space-sick for a while, but usually recover quickly. Then they really enjoy the experience. One side-effect of living on the ISS is that without gravity to hold the bones together, the spine stretches 2 in. (5 cm) or more.

1 A Progress cargo craft brings 4,400 lbs. (2 tonnes) of supplies to the ISS.
2 Preparing a meal in the ISS galley, Zvezda module.
3 Three ISS crew and seven shuttle crew join up to say hello to the camera.
4 Mealtime – spot the tape holding an apple and food floating out of a can.
5 Suited astronauts prepare for EVA in the Quest airlock module.
6 Closeup of Zvezda's galley.
7 Regular exercise on the ISS treadmill is vital for healthy muscles.
8 Astronauts pose for the camera.
9 Working in the Destiny module.
10 Vladimir Deshurov works in his sleep station – note the personal music system on the wall.
11 Keeping Zvezda's cooker working well requires regular maintenance.
12 A vacuum sucks up stray hairs during a haircutting session.

1	2	3
4		5
		6
12	11	10	9	8	7

SPACE JUNK

There are millions of stray particles in space, ranging from tiny bits of space dust to pieces of discarded rocket. If the ISS is hit by something big, there could be a catastrophe.

SPACE DUST DOES NOT SOUND VERY DANGEROUS, but speed is what counts – and most objects are zipping along at 6 miles per second (10 km/sec) or more. Delicate items such as solar panels are most at risk, because an object hitting a panel vaporizes instantly, causing a flash of heat. This may damage the panel, or send a false signal to control equipment. Slightly larger particles, known as meteoroids, are also a danger. Most are tiny, but some are big enough to punch holes in metal.

On the ISS, critical components, such as living areas and high-pressure tanks, are protected by layers of ceramic fiber, providing a "bumper" system that should give protection from objects up to about half an inch (10 mm) or so. Bigger chunks of material can be tracked by Earth-based radar equipment, and in an emergency the ISS could maneuver out of the way.

A bigger danger to the ISS could be visiting spacecraft. In June 1997, a Progress supply spacecraft collided with Russia's space station Mir. The collision nearly caused a disaster – the impact knocked Mir into a spin, and much of the station lost air. But luck was on the cosmonauts' side – vital

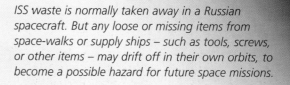

ISS waste is normally taken away in a Russian spacecraft. But any loose or missing items from space-walks or supply ships – such as tools, screws, or other items – may drift off in their own orbits, to become a possible hazard for future space missions.

supplies, including food and water, were in undamaged modules, and eventually repairs were made. Today, the only visitors to the ISS are US Shuttles, and Russian Progress and Soyuz craft. Future plans include robot-guided supply ships from Europe and Japan, so operators checking on movements will have to keep a sharp eye.

The main picture here shows a possible disaster scene, where a discarded fuel tank has collided with the ISS. Modules and docked spacecraft have been sent flying, and the survival of crew and station is at stake.

Big space rocks may seem more frightening than tiny grains of dust, but they are easily spotted, and the ISS has thruster systems to avoid them.

In 1993, a tiny chip of paint hit an Orbiter window. Colliding at 37 miles per second (60 km/sec), it cracked the outer pane.

There are thousands of space objects circling the Earth. The bigger items, such as satellites and empty fuel tanks, can be tracked from Earth. Tiny objects are more difficult to spot, so are more dangerous.

INTO THE FUTURE

The ISS is designed to operate continuously for at least 10 to 15 years, but it is likely to be in space for longer. Its future will be linked to how research projects change over the years, and what new spacecraft will be flying into space.

RESULTS FROM EXPERIMENTS on the ISS may lead to a "high frontier" for space products. For example, new drugs may be made in the free-fall conditions of Earth's orbit. By 2010, there could be plans for a space factory to manufacture products in space. But maintaining the ISS takes a lot of time, and as long as there is only a three-person crew on board, there will be times when keeping the station working comes before an important experiment.

Future plans include an extra docked Soyuz or advanced mini-shuttle, and extra people on the ISS to help with the science experiments.

Entrance hatch

Twin fins keep the craft stable in flight.

Lower surfaces heat up as this future mini-shuttle hits the atmosphere at high speed.

If experiments with making drugs or producing new materials are successful, then a space factory may be assembled near the ISS. Finished goods could be sent to Earth aboard space freighters.

Future spacecraft visiting the ISS should enable full crews of seven to stay on board for months at a time in the knowledge that, should a catastrophe occur, a vehicle would be available for their safe return.

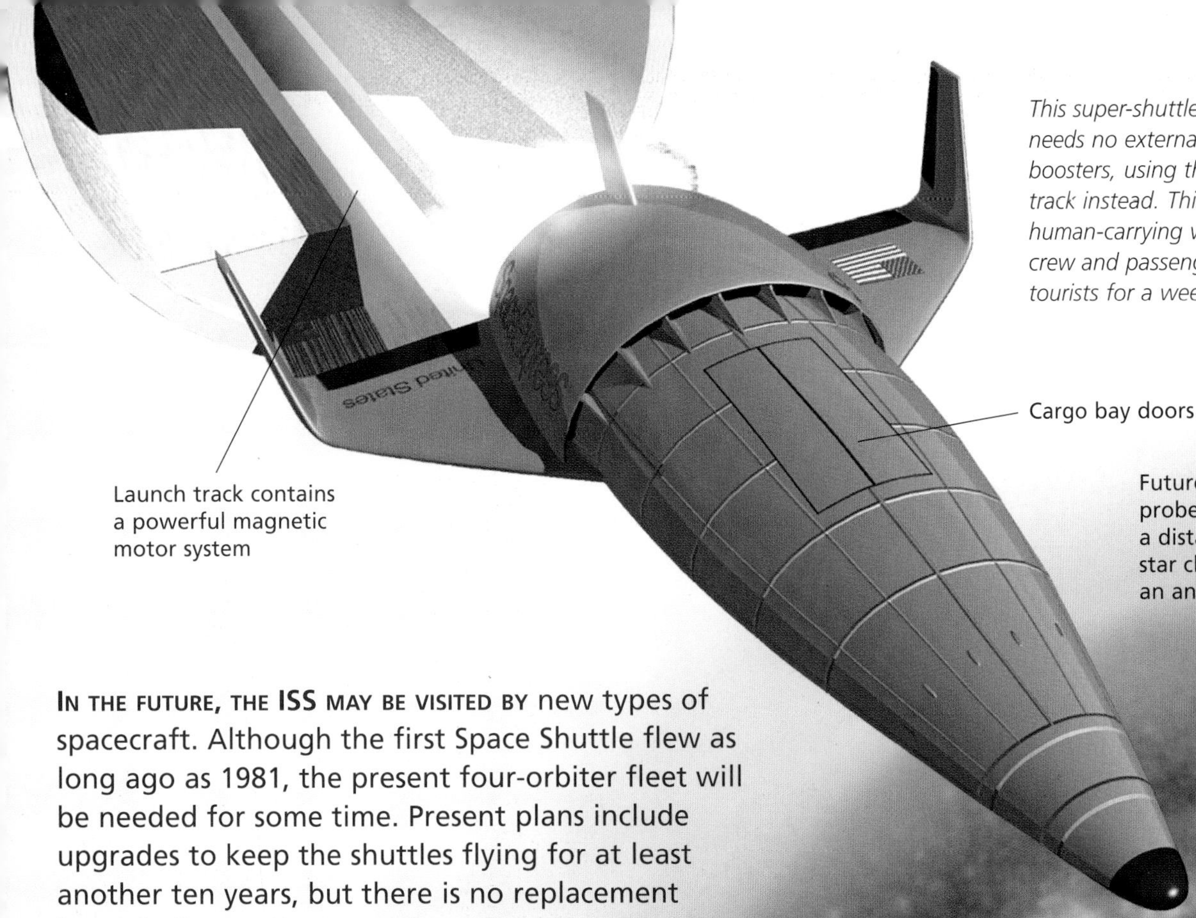

This super-shuttle of the year 2020 needs no external fuel tanks or rocket boosters, using the magnetic launch track instead. This is a cargo craft, but human-carrying versions could carry crew and passengers, even a group of tourists for a week's space vacation.

Cargo bay doors

Launch track contains a powerful magnetic motor system

Future ISS observations will probe deep into space. Here a distant galaxy reveals new star clusters circling around an ancient glowing core.

IN THE FUTURE, THE ISS MAY BE VISITED BY new types of spacecraft. Although the first Space Shuttle flew as long ago as 1981, the present four-orbiter fleet will be needed for some time. Present plans include upgrades to keep the shuttles flying for at least another ten years, but there is no replacement being built yet. However, there are some ideas for new shuttle craft, including the sleek design shown above. This would not leave the ground straight up from a launch pad. Instead, it would be boosted along a special track by magnetic motors, before its own engines cut in for liftoff.

The Chinese Shenzhou craft is based on Russia's Soyuz design.

China's future space plans include crewed flights, building a space station, and even a flight to the Moon by 2010. The Shenzhou spacecraft is launched from Earth on a Long March booster rocket.

Smaller space stations have been built before, but the larger ISS should be completed by 2006.

THE IDEA OF A SPACE STATION is not new – in fact, realistic plans were dreamed up back in the 1950s. But those ideas were for huge wheel-shaped stations that would spin slowly, like giant pinwheels. The concept was that a spin would give the sensation of gravity to people inside. It was a good idea, but a station as advanced as this was not possible then. Nor is it now. Instead, ISS designers went for something that looks similar to stations that were built in the 1970s and 1980s, though much bigger. And importantly, all ISS components are standard-sized items that fit in existing Space Shuttles and Proton rockets. The first part of the ISS placed in orbit was the Zarya module, flown in a Proton rocket in November 1998. It was followed in December by the Unity node. Construction continued rapidly after that, and the first three-person crew went aboard in October 2000. Since then, the ISS has been occupied by new crews at regular intervals. By 2006, the ISS should be complete, and will then be good for many years of science research.

In the 1950s, many scientists thought that a space station would be built as a space-wheel.

1971 SALYUT 1 Russian Salyut 1 is first space station

1973 SKYLAB

2000 POWER Big photovoltaic wings attached

2000 CREW ONE

2001 DESTINY U.S. laboratory module attached

2001 LEONARDO

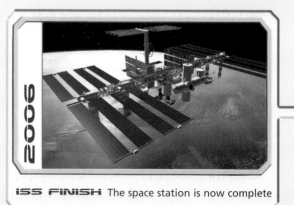

2006 ISS FINISH The space station is now complete

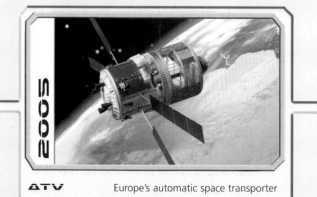

2005 ATV Europe's automatic space transporter

2005 CUPOLA

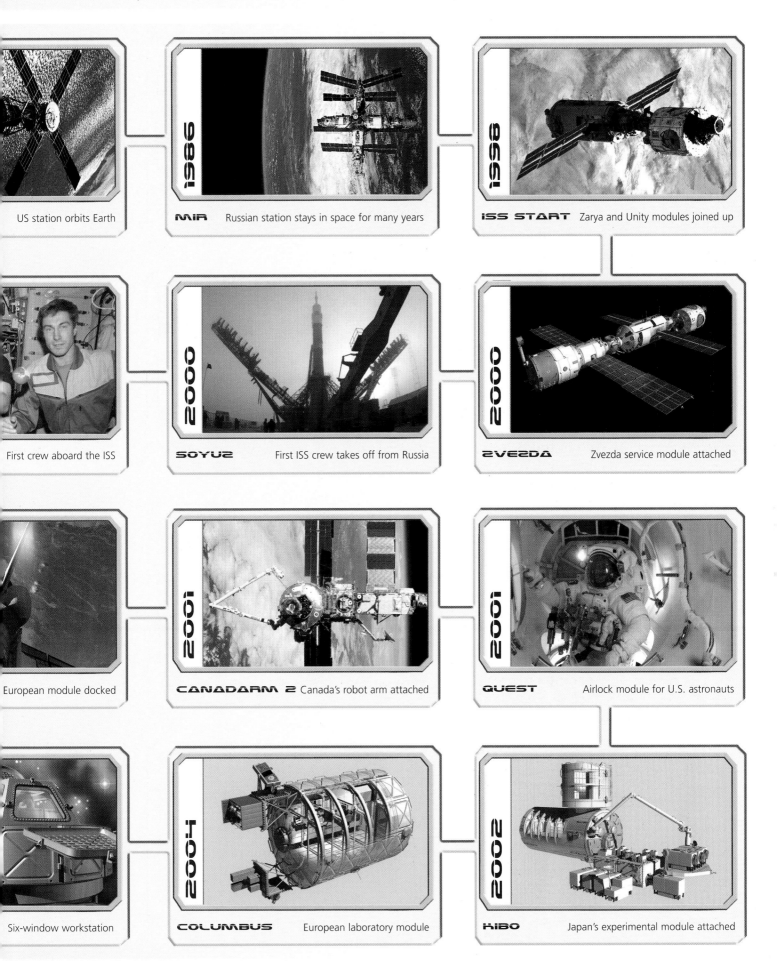

US station orbits Earth

1986 MIR — Russian station stays in space for many years

1998 ISS START — Zarya and Unity modules joined up

First crew aboard the ISS

2000 SOYUZ — First ISS crew takes off from Russia

2000 ZVEZDA — Zvezda service module attached

European module docked

2001 CANADARM 2 — Canada's robot arm attached

2001 QUEST — Airlock module for U.S. astronauts

Six-window workstation

2004 COLUMBUS — European laboratory module

2002 KIBO — Japan's experimental module attached

airlock
A module where crews or materials can pass from a spacecraft to space and back again. There are several of these on the ISS, including the Quest module for US astronauts.

antenna
A device (which may be rod- or dish-shaped) that sends or receives TV and radio signals.

Apollo
Name for the space program that sent astronauts on Moon-landing flights from 1969 to 1972.

atmosphere
The gases that surround a planet. The Earth is made up mainly of the gases nitrogen and oxygen.

attitude jet
Small engine (often gas-powered) that is used for fine adjustments to a spacecraft's heading and angle.

automated transfer vehicle (ATV)
Disposable vehicles, the European-built ATVs will take cargo supplies to the ISS. They will then serve as flying trash cans, taking ISS waste on board and burning up on re-entry in Earth's atmosphere. The ATV was named the Jules Verne in 2002.

Baikonur Cosmodrome
The main space base for launching Soyuz and Progress craft to the ISS.

Canadarm
Canadian-built "robot" arm. One type is used on the shuttle. The larger Canadarm 2 is used on the ISS.

cargo bay
Part of the Space Shuttle that carries satellites, modules, and other equipment into orbit.

centrifuge
A machine that spins around and around. A person or experiment inside can weigh more or less, depending on the speed of rotation.

ceramic fiber
One of the materials used in the meteoroid-protection system installed on ISS modules.

crystal
Any form of solid material with naturally flat sides. Sugar and salt grains are familiar examples.

docking
The meeting and joining of two spacecraft, such as a Russian Soyuz docking with the ISS. A firm connection is called a "hard dock."

docking port
The specific part of a spacecraft used for docking.

European Space Agency (ESA)
A multi-national space research organization backed by several European countries, the European equivalent of NASA.

Express Pallet
Short for EXpedite the PRocessing of Experiments to Space Station, this houses experiments outside the station and is part of Brazil's hardware contribution to the ISS. It can be located by robotic arm anywhere along the central truss.

External Tank (ET)
Tank that holds fuel for the orbiter's main engines.

Extravehicular Activity (EVA)
When an astronaut works outside a spacecraft, floating in space. Also known as a "spacewalk."

foamed metal
Special form of metal that is honeycombed with gas bubbles.

free-fall (weightless)
The term for a "body" – spacecraft or human – in orbit, when it is weightless (because an orbit is technically a "fall" all the way around a planet).

friction heat
Heat caused by molecules of air rubbing against a spacecraft's outer shell as it re-enters the atmosphere at high speed from orbit.

fuel cell
Machine that makes electricity by mixing hydrogen and oxygen. The cell's waste is pure water.

global warming
The increase in the general temperature of the Earth.

gravity
The unseen force that keeps us firmly on the Earth. In orbit, gravity is much less, but it is not exactly "zero." The correct term for orbiting craft and crew is that they are in "free-fall" or "microgravity."

Integrated Truss Assembly (ITA)
Long girder-like structure that is the "backbone" of the ISS.

Kibo (Hope)
Japanese Experimental Module (JEM), a laboratory made in Japan.

manipulator arm
Remote-controlled "robot" arm used to move items around a Space Shuttle and the ISS. Also called a Remote Manipulating System (RMS) or Canadarm.

meteoroid
Small bits of dust and rock particles that fly through space at up to 45 miles per second (72 km/sec).

microgravity
The tiny gravity pull still apparent on an orbiting craft. On the ISS, microgravity is about one-billionth as strong as gravity on Earth.

Mir (Peace)
Russia's last space station. It was designed for a 5-year life, but lasted for 15 years, until March 2001.

module
General name for a major section of a spacecraft. One example is the ISS Destiny laboratory module.

Multi-Purpose Logistics Module (MPLM)
Cylinders used as "moving-trucks" for the ISS. Made in Italy, they are named after famous Italian painters, Raphael, Leonardo, and Donatello.

node
On the ISS, a connector module that joins other modules together.

orbit
The curving path (circular or oval) in space that an object takes around another. It applies to the orbit of our Earth around the Sun, as well as to a spacecraft around the Earth.

Orbiter
Name for the crewed part of the Space Shuttle, but can also be used for any spacecraft that orbits a planet, or the Moon.

orbiting height
The distance of an orbiting object from the main body, also called its "altitude." This height can vary if the

orbit is an oval. The ISS orbits Earth from 220 to 280 mi. (350-450 km).

pallet
On the ISS, a structure that is used as a base for machinery. An example is Kibo's "back porch" pallet, on which experiments can be mounted.

Portable Life Support System (PLSS)
Machinery in a spacesuit backpack that holds air, water, heating, and cooling systems. A PLSS can support an astronaut for eight hours, though most spacewalks don't last that long.

Progress
Russian uncrewed supply craft, developed from the three-seat crewed Soyuz spacecraft.

Proton
Rocket that launches Russian ISS modules and spacecraft into orbit.

radiation
A term for the "electromagnetic spectrum," in which you find light, radio waves, cosmic rays, x-rays, infra-red, and more. If living tissue receives too much radiation, cell damage and cancer may be caused.

radiator
On the ISS, a flat panel that gets rid of waste heat into space.

Salyut 1 (Salute)
The first Russian space station, sent into space in April 1971. Six more Salyuts were later built.

Skylab
First U.S. space station, sent into orbit in May 1973. It was converted from the third stage of a Saturn 5 rocket.

solar panels
Flat panels that convert light energy to electricity. They are used in spacecraft as they provide electrical power by converting sunlight. Also known as a "photovoltaic array."

Soyuz (Union)
Russia's crewed spacecraft. The first Soyuz was flown in 1967. It has been updated constantly since, and is also a lifeboat for the ISS crews.

space station
An orbiting spacecraft that is occupied by crews on a permanent, or semi-permanent basis.

space telescope
A telescope used in space. The best known is the HST or Hubble Space Telescope.

spacesuit
Special clothing worn by astronauts and cosmonauts to protect them from the deadly conditions in space. Breathing, heating, and cooling systems are all required.

thermal control system (TCS)
Fluid-filled tubes for cooling the ISS solar power system, and radiators that disperse heat into space.

thruster rocket
A small rocket used in space to adjust a spacecraft's orbit.

vacuum
Literally, no air. Most of space is a vacuum, although radiation in various forms is always present.

Zarya (Sunrise)
The first ISS module sent into orbit. It was built in Russia, though commissioned by the United States. Zarya is the ISS control center.

INDEX